THIS DAY

LILLIAN DAVIS

This Day

Tellwell Talent
www.tellwell.ca

ISBN
978-0-2288-9498-8 (Paperback)
978-0-2288-9499-5 (eBook)

THIS DAY

31-Days
of
POWERFUL PRAYERS OF

Kingdom Declarations and Decrees
to activate your breakthrough

Self-help books talk about being more positive and improving your mental health. In this case, 31 days of powerful prayers would result in a breakthrough in one's relationship with God or building a closer relationship, or learning how to pray (if one has never done so before).

TABLE OF CONTENTS

ACKNOWLEDGEMENTS

First, I give honor to God for giving me the insight and ability to put pen to paper.

I am grateful that God sees fit to reveal these prayers to me at this time. God has brought some powerful men and women into my life who have encouraged, supported and inspired me to entertain a constant connectivity to Christ. All that they poured into me has inspired me to become a productive servant in God's kingdom.

I want to thank Doctor Pat Francis for her continual encouragement and her faithfulness in preaching the undiluted word of God, which gave me a new lens to see God's Chayil glory. For 29 years, I have been in her ministry, and I dearly love and appreciate her.

Acknowledgement to my friends, Elaine Beckford, Glenda Carty and Jean Cunningham, for being a source of strength and for encouraging me to push ahead. I truly appreciate your daily prayers.

Special thank you to Pastor Benton Gibbons of St. Thomas LifeHouse Church, who graciously embraced and encouraged me into fellowship. Thank you, Pastor, for believing in me.

Lastly, thank you Nathania Davis, my daughter, who never doubted that this book would come to fruition.

Note: *Chayil glory derives from the Hebrew word "chayil' (strength, might, wisdom, wealth, ability, efficiency, powerful) – so, chayil glory is a powerful glory in Christ within believers.*

A NOTE FROM A FRIEND

As a dear friend of Lillian and a believer in Christ, I have seen the daily need for prayers in our lives. There are many prayer books, but this book is unique as this is an inspiration from God to Lillian.

I have known the author for over 15 years. She is a God-fearing person, kind, intelligent and very loving. We became friends while volunteering for an association that provides financial assistance and scholarships for children in the Caribbean.

As a believer in Christ and an ordained minister, Lillian has been a leader in many prayer groups, which have been helpful to people spiritually, physically, and emotionally. I grew up learning how to pray and to use prayer to acquire many answers to challenges and achievements.

I see Lillian as a spiritual coach in our everyday life. Her spiritual insight, intelligence, passion and commitment to God's words are always inspiring. In this book, several prayers are listed for any challenge or change that one needs. The wordings are clear and concise and will provide the tool to challenge the opportunity to create a relationship with the Lord Jesus Christ.

As you learn how to pray by reading this book, your life will be enhanced with God's word, who is our example. Whatever your needs are, and if you trust and believe in God, these prayers will definitely make a difference.

Jean Cunningham

FOREWORD

This book is powerful! Praying and declaring in the name of Jesus for 31 days is a powerful way to do life.

This is a great guide to shift your prayer life in a big way. I found it a benefit having specific areas to read through as I added it to my daily prayer time. It challenged me to think through that area of my life, spirituality, and prayer time as I walked through the 31 days.

I recommend this book to everyone, especially those who want to grow in their walk with God.

Benton Gibbons
Lead Pastor | LifeHouse Church
St. Thomas, Ontario, Canada

INTRODUCTION

You may ask, why pray? Why another book on prayer? The answer is simple. We are commanded to pray and prayer is needed. When we pray, God's grace, power, anointing and revelation are released. Prayer impacts our lives because it is a link to God's power and blessings.

THIS DAY was birthed from my daily prayer journaling with God. On January 26, 2021, God dropped in my spirit to write a prayer on every topic listed in this book. I pray that these life-changing words will have a tremendous impact on your lives.

May your lives overflow with the goodness of God as you read and study these prayers. Make them your personal declarations and believe them to be God's proclamation to carry you through all circumstances of life. The God of more than enough is ready to do great things for you through these prayers.

Dictionary meaning of **Declaration**: *to make something known formally.*

Dictionary meaning of **Decree**: *an official order/legal authority*. You must have authority to issue a decree.

Here are some scriptures on prayer:

Ephesians 1:17: "I keep asking that the God of our Lord Jesus Christ, the glorious Father, may give you the Spirit of wisdom and revelation, so that you may know him better." (NIV)

Job 22:28: "Thou shalt also decree a thing, and it shall be established unto thee: and the light shall shine upon thy ways." (KJV)

Psalms 105:4: "Look to the Lord and his strength; seek his face always." (NIV)

Mark 11:23-24: "I tell you the truth, if anyone says to this mountain, 'Go, throw yourself into the sea,' and does not doubt in his heart but believes that what he says will happen, it will be done for him. Therefore I tell you, whatever you ask for in prayer, believe that you have received it, and it will be yours." (NIV)

Ephesians 6:17-18 "Take the helmet of salvation and the sword of the Spirit, which is the word of God. And pray in the Spirit on all occasions with all kinds of prayers and requests. With this in mind, be alert and always keep praying for all the Lord's people." (NIV)

Matthew 26:41: "Watch and pray, that ye enter not into temptation: the spirit indeed is willing, but the flesh is weak." (KJV)

BENEFITS OF DECLARING GOD'S WORD

When we serve God, we simply acknowledge that there is a God, and we operate in obedience. We extend this service as a form of worship. 1 Peter 4:10-11 states that worship is a way to express gratitude for what Jesus has done for us. The result leads to multi-faceted benefits, which is a special favor or gift given by God to his children that brings happiness and joy to their lives.

As we commune daily with God and align ourselves with his word and engage in worship, praise, thanksgiving, fasting and prayer, we will reap the joy of his benefits.

A WORD FROM THE AUTHOR

I've come to the realization that there are benefits in seeking God for all our circumstances. I know that the benefits of serving God come in many facets. It comes in talking to God daily. It comes in your family being blessed. It comes in just enjoying life with family and friends. It comes in talking to a stranger on the street. The benefits are numerous, and loving and serving God is priceless.

Powerful breakthrough prayers are a special gift given by God to his children, which brings freedom. Praying is serving God. Not only do we serve God, but we serve others through our prayers. As believers in Christ, we have the Holy Spirit in us who speaks to us on a continuous basis so that we can be in alignment with Father, Son and Holy Spirit.

This book is not only for Christians; it is for everyone. I pray this book will have a tremendous impact on every person who reads a prayer from it.

As part of our daily walk, let's be diligent and present ourselves and our situations to God. Our God knows all things, so let's just be open to him so that we can benefit from all that he has for us. There are many aspects of kingdom empowerment that we can work with. To start off, let's be attuned to his voice daily so we can know his will for our lives.

Let's connect afresh with God daily, and if we let him lead us every day, bonds of wickedness will crumble and there will be excess room for expansion in our lives.

LET ME PRAY WITH YOU

Father, as your people read these prayers out loud, I pray that your redemptive blood will cover them and hide them from the plans of the evil one. I pray, Lord Jesus, that your grace will multiply in their lives. I pray, oh God, that you will grant them the desires of their hearts as they share their emotions and feelings with you.

I pray for a deeper relationship with you, God. I pray that you will release your wisdom, courage, power, knowledge and understanding on them in the mighty name of Jesus. God, I pray that they will behold the beauty of your glory, and what you have created, and that they will be filled with your grace and truth in Jesus' name. Amen!

ONE

BLESSINGS

Blessed shalt thou be in the city, and blessed shalt thou be in the field. Deuteronomy 28:3 (KJV)

Father, in the name of Jesus Christ of Nazareth, today I declare blessings upon our lives. I declare blessings in the lives of our children, our families, friends, workplaces, our communities, our churches, our schools, our businesses, our governments, and all that is attached to us in Jesus' Holy Name.

God, in everything that we are involved with, we declare your blessings right now in Jesus' name. I thank you that in Luke 6:38, your word states that you will give to us an overflow of your blessings. Thank you for your endless blessings and help us to walk in them in Jesus' name. Amen!

Luke 6:38 – *Give, and you will receive. Your gift will return to you in full – pressed down, shaken together to make room for more, running over, and poured into your lap. The amount you give will determine the amount you get back.* (NLT)

Reflections/Activities

State what you are praising God for today.

Life - I woke up this morning. Thank you Lord
- my mother, my daughter, roof over my head food to eat
- my 3 true friends - Wilma N., Marjorie B. Marie S.

Write down the names of those you will pray for today.

My daughter, my mother, my nephew André and the rest of my family
- Peace in the World

Write down what would like you see as the results of your prayers.

. Would like to see some restoration in my family
- protection for my nephew André
- my daughter would continue to be prosperous and focused

TWO

CHURCH

And I say also unto thee, that thou art Peter, and upon this rock I will build my church; and the gates of hell shall not prevail against it. Matthew 16:18 (KJV)

Father, **THIS DAY** I bring your church to you in Jesus' name. I thank you that you have called the church in this specific time to advance your kingdom. Thank you for Holy Spirit, who is the seal of our promise to heaven. I thank you for the blood of Jesus Christ, who has redeemed us from sin.

I pray God that revival will come as you raise up your church again to be a people of prayer who bring the good news of salvation to the lost. I pray, oh God, that as your people extend themselves to be used by you, many will be drawn to you, and we will see much fruit in their lives.

Lord, I pray for an outpouring of your spirit on all people. I pray for an awakening in your people. I pray God that there will be an awareness of your love and grace that encase all people. May Holy Spirit stir in your church a desire to know you more and humbly walk with you, in the mighty name of Jesus Christ. Amen!

Reflections/Activities

State what you are praising God for today.

Health

Write down the names of those you will pray for today.

Myself
Nephew - André

Write down what you see as the results of your prayers.

THREE

COUNTRY

Who will not fear you, Lord, and glorify your name? For you alone are holy. All nations will come and worship before you, for your righteous deeds have been revealed. Revelations 15:4 (NLT)

Sovereign Lord, Ruler of heaven and earth, I declare today that you are the God of all ages. I declare that you are Almighty God, and there is no other god above you. Your word says that the earth is yours and all that is within it.

I come **THIS DAY,** and I give my country (name of country) and all countries, particularly those suffering through the hardship of war or drought and famine, over to your lordship right now in the name of Jesus. I ask, oh God, to take over every area of this country. I ask for divine covering over it in the name of Jesus. I ask, dear Lord, to forgive us for not putting you first in the affairs that concern this country. I pray that you will lift up the people of this nation and cause them to turn to you and seek your face.

Thank you for blessing this land, oh Lord, and may you be glorified in this nation in the mighty name of Jesus our Lord. Amen!

Reflections/Activities

State what you are praising God for today.

Write down the names of those you will pray for today.

Write down what you see as the results of your prayers.

FOUR

COURAGE

Be strong in the Lord and in His mighty power. Ephesians 6:10 (NLT)

Father, in the name of Jesus Christ, through faith in you, God, I make a declaration that **THIS DAY**, courage will be anchored in my life. When fear grips me, I pray that courage will step right in and take over in Jesus' name.

Holy Spirit, uproot anything that would want to prevent me from living a courageous life. Give me strength to face every ordeal that comes my way. I thank you, Lord, that you are my true source of strength. Help me to be daring so that when difficulties come, I will tackle them with firmness and boldness.

Father, I declare in the name of Jesus that I am strong and of good courage according to Deuteronomy 31:6 and

Joshua 1:9, and I decree that I am living with unwavering bravery and relentless hope in you. I declare it is done in Jesus' name. Amen!

Reflections/Activities

State what you are praising God for today.

Write down the names of those you will pray for today.

Write down what you see as the results of your prayers.

FIVE

DANGER

A prudent person foresees danger and takes precautions. The simpleton goes blindly on and suffers the consequences. Proverbs 22:3 (NLT)

Mighty God, how great thou art! **THIS DAY**, I decree and declare that no danger shall come near me according to Psalms 91:10. I pray that you will guide and protect everyone who is facing any insecurities, especially if they are any likelihood of danger.

Thank you, Lord, that I am not at risk because I am covered under the blood of Jesus and your grace and mercy overshadows me.

Lord, I thank you that there is no possibility of me suffering any harm or unpleasant things because you are my refuge, and I am secured in you in Jesus' name I pray. Amen!

Reflections/Activities

State what you are praising God for today.

Write down the names of those you will pray for today.

Write down what you see as the results of your prayers.

SIX

EAGERNESS

Lord, give me your unfailing love, the salvation that you promised me. Psalm 119:41 (NLT)

Father, I declare today that my steps are ordered by you. You help me each day to go even further in this journey called life. I thank you for the eagerness to serve you because I want to work for the glory of your kingdom. Thank you for teaching me not to be anxious about anything.

I am grateful that I can be eager to tell others about your goodness in Jesus' name. Amen!

Reflections/Activities

State what you are praising God for today.

Write down the names of those you will pray for today.

Write down what you see as the results of your prayers.

SEVEN

EXCELLENCE

Then Daniel was distinguished because an excellent spirit was in him. Daniel 6:3 (ASV)

Heavenly Father, how excellent is your name in all the earth. I give you thanks, father, for creating the heavens and the earth. Thank you, God, for allowing me to take part in your creation. I thank you that you have given me the opportunity to become a son/daughter through Jesus Christ, who died on the cross for my sins.

Lord God, it is good to know that I am now one with Christ because I have come into alignment with you by making you Lord of my life. Thank you, Lord Jesus, for the good work you did on the cross, and now I can live a joyful life because of your sacrifice and love.

God, you are an excellent father. Your word says in Psalms 8:1&9 how excellent is your name in all the earth.

Surely, your name is majestic and worthy of all honor and praise.

I want to thank you that I can come to you in the name of Jesus, knowing that I have security in your name and that because of your unfailing love for me, you are making me a person of distinction in this life and the world. I thank you, in Jesus' holy name. Amen!

Reflections/Activities

State what you are praising God for today.

Write down the names of those you will pray for today.

Write down what you see as the results of your prayers.

EIGHT

FAMILY

As for me and my house, we will serve the Lord. Joshua 24:15 (KJV)

Father, in the name of Jesus Christ, I declare **THIS DAY** that every stronghold that has come up against our families must come down. I ask, oh God, that you help us to walk in the blessings you have already released over our lives.

I declare that our families will not bow to the enemy. We refuse to bow in the name of Jesus. I pray for a shifting in our families. I pray for a turnaround of every situation that is contrary to your will, Lord.

Every contrary spirit coming against our households causing division and confusion, every undefiled spirit fighting against us, I come against them with the fire of the Holy Spirit. I pray that the power of God will overtake every household in the name of Jesus.

Mighty God, I plea the blood of Jesus, and I take back our minds, our finances, our health, our marriages, our children, our households. We take them back in Jesus' name. Every arrow sent against our families, I intercept them by the blood of Jesus and send them back to the sender in Jesus' name.

Almighty God, those monitoring spirits, I cut them off in the name of Jesus. I thank you, Jesus, that your blood speaks, and no destiny of our loved ones will be aborted in the mighty name of Jesus. Loosen every chain, God. Break every yoke, God, and set free by your power.

I declare that every seed of the enemy is aborted by the fire of the Holy Spirit this very day. I declare that my family is not destined to lose because we are already on the winning side.

Thank you, Lord, that our households are secured in Jesus. Amen!

Reflections/Activities

State what you are praising God for today.

Write down the names of those you will pray for today.

Write down what you see as the results of your prayers.

NINE

FAVOR

May the favor of the Lod our God rest upon us; establish the work of our hands for us – yes, establish the work of our hands. Psalm 90:17 (NIV)

Our father, I thank you today for the favor you show me. I declare that this is my day of extraordinary favor in Jesus' name. I thank you that your grace is more than enough for me. Thank you, Lord God, for the blessings that you are pouring out on me in great measure. I thank you that your glory is moving in my life in Jesus' name.

I declare that **THIS DAY**, your favor will be optimized in all that I do, and the greatness of your FAVOR will follow me all the days of my life. This I declare in Jesus' name. Amen!

Reflections/Activities

State what you are praising God for today.

____
____
____
____
____
____

Write down the names of those you will pray for today.

____
____
____
____
____
____

Write down what you see as the results of your prayers.

____
____
____
____
____
____

TEN

FEAR

For God hath not given us the spirit of fear; but of power, and of love, and of a sound mind. 2 Timothy 1:7 (KJV)

Father in the name of Jesus, I thank you that fear is not a part of my DNA. I thank you that fear has no hold on me. I praise your name, Jesus, that when you were on the cross, you conquered fear.

Today, I place my life in your hands, and I declare in Jesus' name that I have not been given the spirit of fear but of power, love and a sound mind, according to 2 Timothy 1:7.

I thank you, Lord, that I am living in peace, joy and love, and no fear can come near my dwelling because I am protected by the blood of Jesus Christ. This, I pray in Jesus' holy name. Amen!

Reflections/Activities

State what you are praising God for today.

Write down the names of those you will pray for today.

Write down what you see as the results of your prayers.

ELEVEN

GOVERNMENT

Everyone must submit to governing authorities. For all authority comes from God, and those in positions of authority have been placed there by God. Romans 13:1 (NLT)

Father, **THIS DAY**, I pray for the government of this country and all governments over the world. I pray that wisdom will prevail as you direct them to do the right thing at every level.

I pray for all leaders in public services, health care, education, police services, defence services, judicial systems, correctional services, broadcasting services, postal services, energy regulatory systems; all that falls under government, I place them under your care, and I pray that you will lift them up Lord and let your power and your strength engulfed them. I pray special blessings for politicians who are wise themselves and have trusted and competent advisors.

God, I pray for every person involved in all government organizations at every level. I pray, oh God, that they will be opened to your wisdom and guidance in all their responsibilities in Jesus' name. Amen!

Reflections/Activities

State what you are praising God for today.

Write down the names of those you will pray for today.

Write down what you see as the results of your prayers.

TWELVE

GOODNESS

Surely goodness and mercy shall follow me all the days of my life: and I will dwell in the house of the Lord for ever. Psalm 23:6 (KJV)

Father, **THIS DAY**, I thank you that your goodness surrounds me. I thank you for the zeal you have given me to pursue your truth and righteousness. I thank you that because of your goodness in my life, I can do all things through Christ, who gives me strength.

Father, I acknowledge, according to Psalms 23:6 and Romans 8:28, that because of your goodness and love, I will receive constant help and support no matter what happens.

I ask God that I will show goodness and kindness to those I encounter daily so that I can bring you glory. I thank you that I can trust the good father to work in all things for my good in Jesus' name. Amen!

Reflections/Activities

State what you are praising God for today.

Write down the names of those you will pray for today.

Write down what you see as the results of your prayers.

THIRTEEN

GRACE

My grace is sufficient for thee: for my strength is made perfect in weakness. 2 Corinthians 12:9 (KJV)

Heavenly Father, I declare **THIS DAY** that your grace, your unexpected, undeserved, generous, spontaneous gift of divine favor is within me.

I declare and decree that grace is my portion and that grace is operating in my life because, according to Genesis 6:8, I, too, have found grace in your eyes.

I thank you for fresh GRACE in Jesus' holy name. Amen!

Reflections/Activities

State what you are praising God for today.

____
____
____
____
____
____

Write down the names of those you will pray for today.

____
____
____
____
____
____

Write down what you see as the results of your prayers.

____
____
____
____
____
____

FOURTEEN

HEALING

Heal the sick, cleanse the lepers, raise the dead, cast out devils: freely ye have received, freely give. Matthew 10:8 (KJV)

Mighty and ever-living God, I thank you **THIS DAY** that through your son Jesus Christ, healing comes to those who believe. I declare and decree **THIS DAY** that the blood that Jesus shed on the cross for us has healed our bodies of every disease, sickness and infirmity in Jesus' name. I thank you, God, that I am walking in divine health.

I thank you, God, that no sickness shall come upon me a second time according to your word in Nahum 1:9. I thank you, God, that all bad situations concerning our health are now turned around, and we accept your life-flowing virtues in our bodies now in Jesus' name.

Thank you, Lord, that we are free from all manner of ailments because good health is our portion in the mighty name of Jesus Christ we pray. Amen!

Reflections/Activities

State what you are praising God for today.

Write down the names of those you will pray for today.

Write down what you see as the results of your prayers.

FIFTEEN

HEALTH

It is not the healthy who need a doctor,
but the sick. Mark 2:17 (NIV)

Father, I thank you **THIS DAY** that you have told us to take care of our bodies. Thank you that your word is the main guiding force of my life. Thank you for direction and wisdom on how to live my best life ever. Lord, I will respect my body and strive for both bodily and spiritual health.

I thank you, God, for the consciousness and the awareness that I am a seed of the Lord. Father, according to Proverbs 17:22, a cheerful and generous heart is good medicine, so please keep me joyful so that my mind, body, emotion and soul will remain healthy all my days.

I thank you that I am free from illness or injury and that wholeness surrounds me in Jesus' mighty name. Amen!

Reflections/Activities

State what you are praising God for today.

Write down the names of those you will pray for today.

Write down what you see as the results of your prayers.

SIXTEEN

JOBS

For the kingdom of heaven is like a landowner who went out early in the morning to hire workers for his vineyard. Mathew 20:1 (NIV)

Abba, father, I come to you in the name of Jesus. I ask for fresh grace and mercy today, Lord. Thank you, God, that you have given us strength, power and authority to overcome every obstacle we will ever face. Lord, I just want to thank you for the job you have given me. Thank you for placing me in the job marketplace at this time.

Help me to shine my light in every dark place at this worksite. Help me to be strong and do my work with excellence as onto you. I thank you, God, for the many opportunities you have given me at work to excel.

Thank you, Lord, that you have aligned me with the right mentors, supervisors and managers so that I can operate at my optimum in the things you have called me to do. I ask, oh Lord, that you will provide these leaders with the right words to say that will encourage and enable me to make good decisions.

Thank you, God, that I was created for great glory because you have planted seeds of greatness in me. Thank you, father, for equipping me and empowering me for greater things ahead.

Lord, and for those without jobs, I pray that you will go before them and prepare the hearts of the people they will be working with to receive them in the name of Jesus. I thank you, Lord, that you are opening doors right now for them and I come against any opposition in the mighty name of Jesus. Amen!

Reflections/Activities

State what you are praising God for today.

Write down the names of those you will pray for today.

Write down what you see as the results of your prayers.

SEVENTEEN

JOY

Rejoice in the Lord always. I will say it again: Rejoice! Philippians 4:4 (NIV)

Father, I want to thank you that your word says in Nehemiah 8:10 that the JOY of the Lord is my strength. I thank you for your strength which never fails. I thank you that all my weaknesses you turn into strengths so that I can be empowered to live life at its maximum in victory through Jesus Christ.

I declare that because I have your JOY, I can withstand the pressures of life because you have given me the power to resist these forces.

I thank you that I am truly living in your JOY, which gives me strength to endure in Jesus' name. Amen!

Reflections/Activities

State what you are praising God for today.

Write down the names of those you will pray for today.

Write down what you see as the results of your prayers.

EIGHTEEN

LONELINESS

Turn to me and be gracious to me, for I am lonely and afflicted. Psalm 25:16 (NIV)

Father, in the name of Jesus, I bring all those who are feeling isolated, sad, depressed, abandoned and lonely to you **THIS DAY**. I thank you, oh God, that you are their companion. Thank you, Lord, that it is said in your word that you will never leave or forsake them. Thank you that you are our present help in times of trouble. I pray, God, that you will reveal yourself to them. I pray, God, that you will send friendships and help.

I pray, oh God, that they will recognize that you are their help and that you will never leave them for one moment. I am thankful that you are always near and that you are their constant friend who is always by their side.

Lord, I thank you that the person reading this prayer recognizes that you love them very much and that you do not want them to feel alone. Thank you, Lord, that you want them to know that, regardless of the situation they are in, you are with them.

Lord, I ask that you cover them with your peace. I ask that you place your hand of comfort on them so they can feel the warmth of your embrace and love in Jesus' holy name. Amen!

Reflections/Activities

State what you are praising God for today.

____

____

____

____

____

____

Write down the names of those you will pray for today.

____

____

____

____

____

____

Write down what you see as the results of your prayers.

____

____

____

____

____

____

NINETEEN

LOVE

Your love for one another will prove to the world that you are my disciples. John 13:35 (NLT)

Father, in the name of Jesus, I declare that I am living a life of victory every day. Abba, father, I truly adore you. Thank you, Lord, for the gift of love. I am grateful that you enable me to feel, experience and demonstrate such a wonderful thing as LOVE. I thank you that through your love, you want me to experience a life of success every day. You are such an awesome God.

I pray, almighty God, that as you continue to instill your love in me, I will be able to show others your love.

Father, let your love flow out of me so that the world around me may know the true love of Jesus Christ this very day. I pray and declare these things in Jesus' holy name. Amen!

Reflections/Activities

State what you are praising God for today.

Write down the names of those you will pray for today.

Write down what you see as the results of your prayers.

TWENTY

MONEY

Money is the answer for everything. Ecclesiastes 10:19 (NIV)

Father God, you said in your word in Ecclesiastes 10:19 that money is the answer for everything. God, you also said in Deuteronomy 8:18 that you have given your people the ability to create wealth. I want to thank you for the wisdom you have given us to be good stewards of what you have entrusted to us.

I thank you that you will help us to use money to accomplish the things you want for us and to help others in need. Thank you that your kingdom will come in our lives as we seek you and use money as a tool to effectively further your kingdom in Jesus' name. Amen!

Reflections/Activities

State what you are praising God for today.

Write down the names of those you will pray for today.

Write down what you see as the results of your prayers.

TWENTY-ONE

PEACE

For Christ himself has brought peace to us. He united Jews and Gentiles into one people when, in his own body on the cross, he broke down the wall of hostility that separated us. Ephesians 2:14 (NLT)

Heavenly Father, it is an honor to declare that **THIS DAY** your peace surrounds me. **THIS DAY**, I declare that you are my living peace.

Father, I thank you that I am covered under the peace of almighty God. Thank you for setting up a banner of peace over me every day of my life.

God, at times I do not understand it all, but I know in spite of everything that may beset me, your peace stands firm, and it calms my wildest fears and puts every anxiety and doubt out of my thoughts.

Because of your heavenly peace that is carrying me each day, I can rest assured that all is well in Jesus' name. Amen!

Reflections/Activities

State what you are praising God for today.

____
____
____
____
____
____

Write down the names of those you will pray for today.

____
____
____
____
____
____

Write down what you see as the results of your prayers.

____
____
____
____
____
____

TWENTY-TWO

PURPOSE

I cry out to God Most High, to God who will fulfill his purpose for me. Psalm 57:2 (NLT)

Father God, I thank you that I have a purpose. Thank you that through your grace, you have designed my life with a divine plan. Your word says in Jeremiah that you have a plan to prosper me. Help me, oh Lord, to find the grace to understand it and to recognize it as something you want for me to experience.

Thank you, God, that the purpose you have for me is being exposed and explored in Jesus' name. I declare that I am operating in my godly purpose to fulfill all the requirements of the life you have for me in Jesus' mighty name. Amen!

Reflections/Activities

State what you are praising God for today.

____

____

____

____

____

____

Write down the names of those you will pray for today.

____

____

____

____

____

____

Write down what you see as the results of your prayers.

____

____

____

____

____

____

TWENTY-THREE

QUIETNESS

Be still, and know that I am God. Psalm 46:10 (NIV)

I thank you **THIS DAY,** Lord Jesus, that I can come into the quietness of your presence and be still before you.

Lord, sometimes it is so difficult to come into a place of quietness because of all the chaos and turmoil around us. At times our lives become so busy that it is hard to find a quiet time or place with you.

Today, God, I thank you that you have given me the space and time to come before you in quietness so that I can seek your face and reflect on your goodness. I thank you that I can listen keenly and hear your voice in the absence of noise. Thank you for the joy that peace brings. Father, being in your presence sometimes requires us to be still and to let you take over, and for that I am grateful.

I am thankful, God, that I am in a place of calmness which enables me to respond appropriately to the things that need my attention. It gives me joy to know that I can have a conversation with you when I shut out all the distractions around me.

Thank you, Lord, for showing me that I truly need alone time with you so that I can flourish. I give you praise, God, and all my love, honor and adoration belongs to you in Jesus' name, I pray. Amen!

Reflections/Activities

State what you are praising God for today.

Write down the names of those you will pray for today.

Write down what you see as the results of your prayers.

TWENTY-FOUR

REST

Come to me, all you who are weary and burdened, and I will give you rest. Mathew 11:28 (NIV)

Lord, today I declare that I am grounded in you and you are my anchor. I am grateful that I can find rest in you. Lord, I thank you that whenever I want to take time out from the things that come my way to throw me off course, I can rest assured that your love covers me.

I am filled with gratitude that I can find peace and assurance in you by resting in your promises knowing that you are always there for me.

Thank you, Lord, that I can sit at your feet, commune with you and find sweet rest in Jesus' name. Amen!

Reflections/Activities

State what you are praising God for today.

Write down the names of those you will pray for today.

Write down what you see as the results of your prayers.

TWENTY-FIVE

SELF-WORTH

I praise you because I am fearfully and wonderfully made. Psalm 139:14 (NIV)

Almighty God, I am grateful that you have embedded in us that we are fearfully and wonderfully made according to Psalms 139:14.

I am thankful that from creation, you made all things good because we are made in your image and likeness, and we are destined for greatness.

Thank you that we are covered in your blood, filled with your spirit, and therefore, we are worth it because your life-given blood, love and grace is flowing in and through us in Jesus' name. Amen!

Reflections/Activities

State what you are praising God for today.

Write down the names of those you will pray for today.

Write down what you see as the results of your prayers.

TWENTY-SIX

TROUBLE

For in the day of trouble he will keep me safe in his dwelling; he will hide me in the shelter of his tabernacle and set me high upon a rock. Psalms 27:5 (NIV)

Heavenly Father, in Psalms 8:4, you said that you are mindful of your people. You also said in your word that disappointments will come, but we should hand over our troubles to you and you will deliver us out of them all. Your word also says you will always be with us and never leave us.

Today, God, I take courage in knowing that although life is rough and rocky right now, you are still here. I thank you that though the wind is fierce, and the water is deep, and there is trouble all around, you have surrounded me on every side with your love, grace and mercy. Thank you that every concern I have, you know of them, and you have already dispatched angel armies to come to my rescue.

I thank you, God, that in spite of all that I am going through, with your divine help, I will come out strong in Jesus' name. Amen!

Reflections/Activities

State what you are praising God for today.

Write down the names of those you will pray for today.

Write down what you see as the results of your prayers.

TWENTY-SEVEN

TRUTH

I am the way, the truth, and the life: no man cometh unto the Father, but by me. John 14:6 (KJV)

Father, in the name of Jesus, I thank you that your truth propels me, and everything is hinged on your truth. Abba, father, it is an honor to know and operate in your truth.

Surely you are the way, the truth, and the life. Thank you for putting your truth before me each day. Thank you for the yearning and the zeal that you have placed in my heart to seek out your truthfulness.

Thank you, God, for new encounters with Holy Spirit every day. I thank you for allowing me to pursue your truth with a new consciousness and desire. Thank you for clothing me with your truth, almighty God. Amen!

Reflections/Activities

State what you are praising God for today.

Write down the names of those you will pray for today.

Write down what you see as the results of your prayers.

TWENTY-EIGHT

UNIQUENESS

I knew you before I formed you in your mother's womb. Jeremiah 1:5 (NLT)

Father in heaven, I thank you today that I am fearfully and wonderfully made. I thank you for your awesomeness that before I was formed in my mother's womb, you knew me according to Jeremiah 1:5. Thank you, God, for your endless love and amazing grace given to us daily.

You took me out of sin and put me in a place of divine purpose, and for that, I am grateful. It is an honor to know that I was made and fashioned in the likeness and image of you, God. Thank you, God, that you made me special, so exceptional that you counted every hair on my head.

Lord, you are great, and I am so grateful that you made me the way I am for a purpose. I thank you for all the wonderful gifts and talents you have placed in my life;

and for the family and friends you have surrounded me with. All that I am, God, is because of you, so I want to give thanks and honor to you for creating me just the way I am, an original masterpiece. In Jesus' name, I pray. Amen!

Reflections/Activities

State what you are praising God for today.

Write down the names of those you will pray for today.

Write down what you see as the results of your prayers.

TWENTY-NINE

VALUE

For physical training is of some value, but godliness is of value in everything and in every way. 1 Timothy 4:8 (AMP)

Heavenly father, I come to you in the name of Jesus, giving thanks for the value you place on me. It is truly wonderful to know that I am valuable and that you see merit in all your people. I am thankful that you have taught us to value each other.

I thank you that we all have something of worth to help each other in many aspects of our lives. Thank you, Lord, that valuing each other is precious to you, and because we choose to do so, your blessings and generous favor will continue to be a part of our lives.

Thank you, Lord, for instilling good principles in us and for helping us to be valuable citizens in society and of your kingdom in Jesus' name. Amen!

Reflections/Activities

State what you are praising God for today.

Write down the names of those you will pray for today.

Write down what you see as the results of your prayers.

THIRTY

WISDOM

The fear of the Lord is the beginning of wisdom, and knowledge of the Holy One is understanding. Proverbs 9:10 (NIV)

Father, it gives me joy that I can come to you in Jesus' name. I speak peace over my life right now in the mighty name of Jesus. I declare **THIS DAY** that I am covered under the blood of Jesus Christ.

I thank you, Father God, that wisdom is a fundamental principle in which we ought to operate. You said if we ask, we shall receive. At times, Lord, we have asked, but we do not receive according to our asking. Help us to know you more, Lord. Crown us with godly wisdom so that we can truly understand your ways.

I declare that I am walking in your divine wisdom because it is the desire of my heart and you grant my requests. I thank you that your wisdom is all around me.

Thank you for letting your wisdom reign in my life in Jesus' holy name. Amen!

Reflections/Activities

State what you are praising God for today.

____

____

____

____

____

____

Write down the names of those you will pray for today.

____

____

____

____

____

____

Write down what you see as the results of your prayers.

____

____

____

____

____

____

THIRTY-ONE

WORRY

Do not be anxious about anything, but in everything, by prayer and petition, with thanksgiving, present your requests to God. Philippians 4:6 (NIV)

Father God, in the name of Jesus Christ, I come to you **THIS DAY** and I declare that I am hidden under your canopy of grace, favor and mercy.

THIS DAY I cast worry aside, and I raise a hallelujah to you, almighty God, because I know that once I am in you, worry has no hold on me and that you carry all my worries for me.

In Matthew 6: 25-34, you said that I should not worry about anything, but I should cast all cares on you. I claim freedom, and I thank you for your delivering power. I declare and decree that I am free, and I am walking in your greatness because worry is defeated in Jesus' name. Amen!

Reflections/Activities

State what you are praising God for today.

Write down the names of those you will pray for today.

Write down what you see as the results of your prayers.

NOTE:

Remember to pray for everyone on your list and meditate on all that you have written. God Bless You!

ABOUT THE AUTHOR

LILLIAN DAVIS is foremost a Christian believer in the Lord Jesus Christ. She is a Kingdom Entrepreneur who owns and operates Dominion Conflict Resolutions Service in Ontario, Canada.

By profession, she is a trained mediator and investigator who specializes in workplace conflicts. She believes her purpose on earth is to advance God's Kingdom. Lillian is an ordained Christian Clergy.

She holds a master's degree in Theology. Lillian has a heart that is willing to serve, and she believes that she is mandated by Mathew 28:18-20 where God's people are promised authority and power to proclaim the gospel throughout the world.

Lillian believes that reaching those who have not yet accepted Jesus Christ as their Lord and Savior is paramount. She believes that Christians should endeavour to fulfill the great commission of Christ, and one way to do so is to make his word known through prayer.

According to the author, she believes that by declaring God's words, lives will be transformed by the power of God, and many will see breakthroughs which will cause them to live a life of success. It is her utmost belief that prayer can change circumstances and that it should be embedded in the life of every person.

NOTES

Manufactured by Amazon.ca
Bolton, ON

36781336R00065